DATE DUE		
100 1/29/18			

COMMUNITY · CONNECTIONS

?

HOW DID THEY BUILD THAT?
HOUSE

BY NANCY ROBINSON MASTERS

3 9082 13373 3785

Published in the United States of America by Cherry Lake Publishing
Ann Arbor, Michigan
www.cherrylakepublishing.com

Content Adviser: Chad Blankenbaker, President, Blank & Baker
Construction Management

Photo Credits: Cover, ©Linda Johnsonbaugh/Shutterstock, Inc.; page 5, ©V. J. Matthew/
Shutterstock, Inc.; page 7, ©benicce/Shutterstock, Inc.; page 9, ©Pincasso/Shutterstock, Inc.;
pages 11 and 13, ©iStockphoto.com/jhorrocks; page 15, ©iStockphoto.com/LifeJourneys;
page 17, ©iStockphoto.com/ArtBoyMB; page 19, ©Lisa F. Young/Shutterstock, Inc.; page 21,
©iStockphoto.com/viki2win

LIBRARY OF CONGRESS CATALOGING-IN-PUBLICATION DATA
Masters, Nancy Robinson.
  How did they build that? House/by Nancy Robinson Masters.
      p. cm.—(Community connections)
  Includes bibliographical references and index.
  ISBN-13: 978-1-60279-982-0 (lib. bdg.)
  ISBN-10: 1-60279-982-2 (lib. bdg.)
  1. House construction—Juvenile literature. 2. Dwellings—Juvenile
literature. I. Title. II. Title: House.
  TH4811.5.M375 2011
  690'.837—dc22   2010030574

Cherry Lake Publishing would like to acknowledge the
work of The Partnership for 21st Century Skills. Please
visit www.21stcenturyskills.org for more information.

Printed in the United States of America
Corporate Graphics Inc.
January 2011
CLSP08

CONTENTS

HOW DID THEY BUILD THAT?

KINDS OF HOUSES

People live in different kinds of houses. Some people live in houses built for one family. Apartments are homes that are joined together under one roof. Mobile homes are homes on wheels. They can be moved. **Modular houses** are built of pieces made in factories. The pieces are put together at a homesite.

Apartments are homes that share the same roof.

Homesites are pieces of land on which homes are built. A homesite may be on a street. It may be close to a lake. It could even be under the ground! Most houses are built to stay in one place.

Modular houses are built with large pieces made in factories.

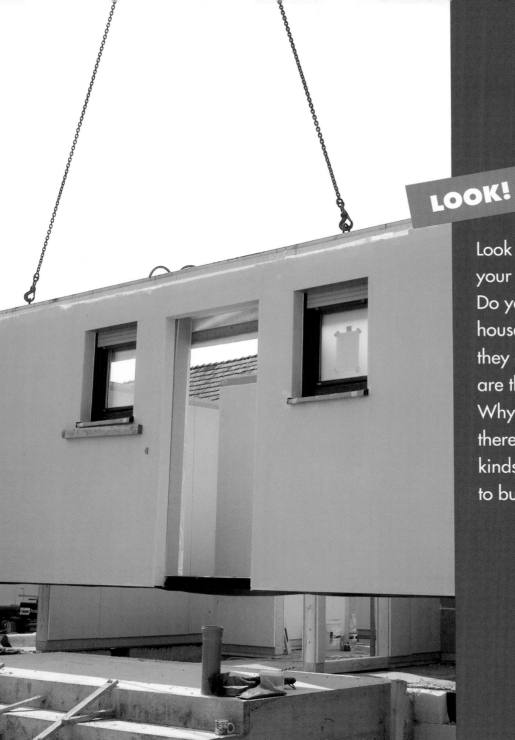

LOOK!

Look around on your way to school. Do you see many houses? How are they alike? How are they different? Why do you think there are different kinds of houses to build?

BEFORE BUILDING

A builder decides where to build a house. He also decides how big the house should be. Then the builder chooses a floor plan. A floor plan is a drawing. It shows the inside of a building without the roof. It shows where each room, window, and door should go.

Floor plans show where each room, window and door will be.

An **architect** makes **blueprints** for the house. Blueprints are drawings of a building. They show more details than floor plans.

Blueprints show where pipes and wires are placed in the walls. They show how the walls and roof join together. They explain which **building materials** to use.

Blueprints are drawings with directions for building a house.

Builders must follow building codes. Building codes are rules for people who work in construction. These rules help make sure builders put up strong and safe houses.

Builders must be sure they follow the rules for building strong, safe houses.

Draw a plan for a house you might like to build someday. What would it look like? Do you think houses in the future will look very different? Use your imagination!

13

FROM THE GROUND UP

A **general contractor** is responsible for building the house. He makes sure the work is done in the right order.

   Foundation crews make the ground flat and even. They build **forms** and pour **concrete** over sand and steel inside the forms.

Cement is poured into forms to build the foundation.

Framing crews build the walls. They build the walls on the ground and then stand them in place. They also help build the roof.

Insulation crews put insulation inside the walls and ceilings. Insulation helps keep houses warm in the winter and cool in the summer.

The frame is like the house's skeleton.

Plumbers lay pipes. They set bathtubs and sinks in place. Electricians run wires to each room. They also put light switches and outlets for plugs in the walls.

Workers may lay bricks over the outside walls. They may also use other materials to cover the outside of the house.

Plumbers place pipes inside the walls of the house.

Carpenters hang doors and windows. Finish crews paint the walls and ceilings. They install cabinets. Tile and carpet crews put floor coverings in place.

Building **inspectors** make sure the house is safe and meets all building codes. The house is ready to live in!

Finish crews put cabinets in a house.

Why must work crews do their jobs in a certain order? Think about it. What if walls were covered before pipes were put in place?

GLOSSARY

architect (AR-kih-tekt) a person who designs buildings

blueprints (BLOO-printss) detailed drawings of a building

building materials (BIL-ding muh-TIHR-ee-uhlz) things used to build, such as bricks and lumber

concrete (KON-kreet) a special mix of sand, cement, water, and tiny stones

forms (FORMZ) frames in which concrete is poured to set

foundation (foun-DAY-shuhn) the solid base of a building

general contractor (JEN-uh-ruhl KON-trak-tur) the person who organizes the parts of a building job

inspectors (in-SPEK-turz) people who check to make sure set rules are followed

insulation (in-suh-LAY-shuhn) material used to keep heat from escaping

modular houses (MAH-juh-lur HOUSS-ihz) houses built in pieces in factories

FIND OUT MORE

BOOKS

Adamson, Heather. *Homes in Many Cultures*. Mankato, MN: Capstone Press, 2008.

Macken, JoAnn Early. *Building a House*. Mankato, MN: Capstone Press, 2009.

WEB SITES

Bureau of Labor Statistics—Architect
www.bls.gov/k12/build04.htm
Architects have cool jobs! Learn more about them here.

PBS KIDS Sprout—Online Kids Games
www.sproutonline.com/sprout/games
Click on the Bob the Builder button to play games and design a simple house.

INDEX

ABOUT THE AUTHOR

Nancy Robinson Masters is the author of more than 35 books. She is also an airplane pilot. She and her husband, Bill, have built three houses. Each of their houses has a room with bookshelves on the walls. Can you guess why?

24